TIMELINES
OF ANCIENT CIVILIZATIONS

EGYPT

David and Patricia Armentrout

Rourke
Publishing LLC
Vero Beach, Florida 32964

© 2004 Rourke Publishing LLC

www.rourkepublishing.com

PHOTO CREDITS: © Peter Langer Associated Media Group pp 14, 23; © Map by Artville; © Corel Corporation all other images

Title page: *King Tutankhamun's gold throne is beautifully decorated.*

Editor: Frank Sloan

Cover and interior design by Nicola Stratford

Library of Congress Cataloging-in-Publication Data

Armentrout, David, 1962-
  Egypt / David and Patricia Armentrout.
    v. cm. — (Timelines of ancient civilizations)
Includes bibliographical references and index.
Contents: 3100-30 B.C. ancient Egypt — 3100-30 B.C. Egyptian myths — 3100-30 B.C. A rich heritage — 3250 B.C. written language — 3250 B.C. Egyptian society — 2686-2181 B.C. Time of the pyramids — 2500 B.C. The Great Sphinx — 2500 BC Mummies — 1570-1200 B.C. The Valley of the Kings — 1503 B.C. Women of power — 1361 B.C. King Tutankhamun — 332-30 B.C. The end of a great empire — Timeline.
  ISBN 1-58952-720-8 (hardcover)
  1. Egypt—Civilization—To 332 B.C.—Juvenile literature. [1. Egypt—Civilization—To 332 B.C.—Chronology.] I. Armentrout, Patricia, 1960- II. Title. III. Series: Armentrout, David, 1962- Timelines of ancient civilizations.
  DT61.A78 2003
  932'.002'02—dc21
                                                    2003001758

Printed in the USA

CG/CG

Contents

ANCIENT EGYPT

The Nile River runs through Egypt. The annual flooding of the Nile creates a sliver of fertile land in the middle of a dry desert. The people of the river valley depend on the nutrient-rich water for food, transportation, and power. It has always been that way, at least since people began to settle along the Nile around 5500 BC.

When **archaeologists** speak of ancient Egypt, they refer to a time when Egypt was controlled by ruling families known as dynasties. Historians believe the first dynasty began around 3100 BC. Archaeologists have learned about ancient Egypt by studying **artifacts** found along the Nile River.

3100-30 BC

3250 BC

2686-2181 BC

2500 BC

1570-1200 BC

1503 BC

1361 BC

332-30 BC

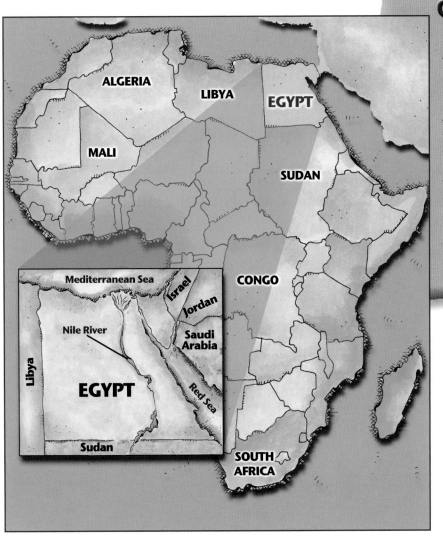

The Nile River is the longest river in the world—4,132 miles (6,650 km).

EGYPTIAN MYTHS

The ancient Egyptians believed gods and goddesses controlled everything in their lives. Each god or goddess had a special job.

Myths are stories that help explain things that people do not understand. Many myths were created by the ancient Egyptians.

One myth explains how the world was created. In this version of the myth, Ra (or Atum), the sun god, came out of an egg that appeared on the water's surface. Ra created Shu, the god of air, and Tefnut, the goddess of moisture. Together Shu and Tefnut became the atmosphere.

They created Geb, the god of earth, and Nut, the goddess of sky. Shu and Tefnut stood on Geb and lifted Nut, who became the sky.

The ancient Egyptians carved images and hieroglyphic messages on tombs and temples.

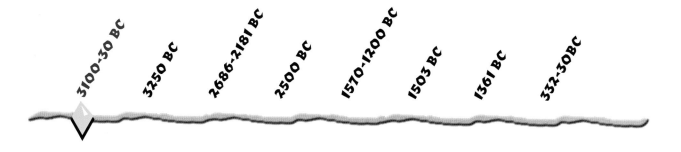

3100-30 BC   3250 BC   2686-2181 BC   2500 BC   1570-1200 BC   1503 BC   1361 BC   332-30 BC

A RICH HERITAGE

There are many reasons ancient Egypt sparks the imagination of so many. The people of ancient Egypt built one of the world's first and longest lasting **civilizations**. Their culture contributed much to our modern way of life.

Ancient Egyptians were among the first to use written language. Their 365-day calendar was remarkably accurate. They also invented the first clocks more than 4,000 years ago.

Egyptian art and architecture influenced artists around the world. Famous structures such as the pyramids, built thousands of years ago, still stand today.

The huge temple at Abu Simbel was carved into the rock for Pharaoh Ramses II.

WRITTEN LANGUAGE

The Egyptians used several forms of writing, or script. The first form, called **hieroglyphics**, was in use before the first dynasty. Hieroglyphics are pictures and symbols. Specially trained Egyptians called **scribes** learned to draw the complicated pictures.

3100-30 BC 3250 BC 2686-2181 BC 2500 BC 1570-1200 BC 1503 BC 1361 BC 332-30 BC

Hieroglyphics were used to mark temples and decorate pottery and stone carvings.

The Egyptians also used two other forms of writing, **hieratic** and **demotic**. Hieratic and demotic were simpler and easier to understand. Hieratic and demotic scripts were used to write letters and prepare legal documents.

In 1799 French soldiers stationed in Egypt found the Rosetta stone. The ancient stone was inscribed with hieroglyphics, demotic, and Greek symbols. An archaeologist was able to translate the symbols. Scientists are now able to read ancient Egyptian writings.

Scribes held a place of honor in Egyptian society.

EGYPTIAN SOCIETY

Ancient Egyptian society was highly developed. At the top of Egyptian society were the **pharaohs**. Next came the priests and priestesses who were often related to the pharaoh. Important officials and scribes were next in line. They ran the day-to-day business of Egypt. Soldiers, craftsmen, and artists who

3100-30 BC

3250 BC

2686-2181 BC

2500 BC

1570-1200 BC

1503 BC

1361 BC

332-30 BC

created many of the artifacts we see today also held a place of honor in society.

At the bottom of society were farmers, laborers, and slaves. Even these lower level members of society had rights. They were treated reasonably well compared to other civilizations. Ancient Egyptians understood the contributions made by these hard-working people.

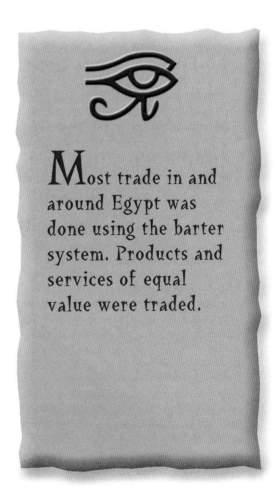

Most trade in and around Egypt was done using the barter system. Products and services of equal value were traded.

Images of everyday life were often depicted on ancient tombs.

13

2686~2181 BC

TIME OF THE PYRAMIDS

The pyramids are giant tombs built for pharaohs. Gold and other treasures were buried with the pharaohs in the belief they could be used in the afterlife.

Most pyramids were built between 2686 BC and 2181 BC during the time known as the Old Kingdom.

3100-30 BC   3250 BC   2686-2181 BC   2500 BC   1570-1200 BC   1503 BC   1361 BC   332-30 BC

The largest pyramid is the Great Pyramid at Giza, Egypt. It was built for king Khufu around 2550 BC. Originally, it stood 482 feet (147 meters) high. It contains more than 2.3 million limestone blocks, each weighing at least 2.5 tons.

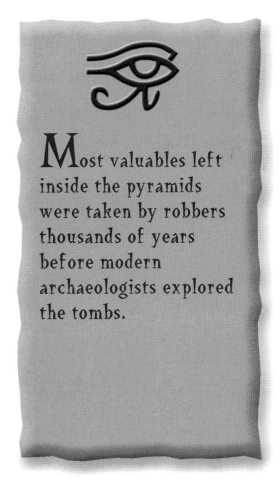

Most valuables left inside the pyramids were taken by robbers thousands of years before modern archaeologists explored the tombs.

The pyramids of Egypt are one of the seven wonders of the ancient world.

2500 BC

THE GREAT SPHINX

The sphinx has recently undergone a renovation project to repair crumbling rock.

Egypt has many famous structures and sculptures. One familiar sculpture is the Great Sphinx.

A sphinx is a mythical creature with the body of a lion and the head of a man.

The Great Sphinx is 69 feet (21 m) tall and 243 feet (74 m) long. The stone beast was carved around 2500 BC. Historians believe it was built to guard king Khafra's pyramid.

Much of the Sphinx was covered by drifting sand for hundreds of years before it was finally dug out.

The Sphinx has obvious damage to the face, especially the nose. The damage may be the result of target practice by soldiers hundreds of years ago.

2500 BC

MUMMIES

Mummies have a modern reputation of being scary and evil. To Ancient Egyptians, however, mummies were a source of comfort to the families of those who had died.

Mummies are the preserved bodies of people or animals. Ancient Egyptians believed that when a person died, he or she would need their bodies in order to pass safely into the afterlife.

After a person died, their organs were removed. The organs were dried, wrapped in linen, and then placed in special jars. The body was stuffed and covered with **natron**, a salty substance that dried the body out.

After several weeks, the natron was removed, revealing a dried shrunken body. The body was then rubbed with herbs and wrapped with many layers of bandages.

Elaborate jars were used to store the organs of the dead.

19

THE VALLEY OF THE KINGS

Pyramids, as awesome as they are, had one big drawback. Because they were so big and so well known, they were often the target of thieves.

3100-30 BC   3250 BC   2686-2181 BC   2500 BC   1570-1200 BC   1503 BC   1361 BC   332-30BC

Starting around 1570 BC, pharaohs were buried in tombs in a secret guarded valley called the Valley of the Kings. Tombs were cut into the sides of cliffs. The tombs were made up of long corridors with separate chambers. It was hoped that the tombs would be safe from thieves. Despite their secret location, most of these tombs were also eventually robbed.

The Valley of the Kings is the home of more than 60 royal tombs.

21

WOMEN OF POWER

The rulers of ancient Egypt were almost always men. The king's throne was usually passed down to his eldest son. Queens, however, were not without power. In a few cases women commanded as much power as men did.

Queen Hatshepsut was one such woman. When her husband the king died, his eldest son was too young to rule. Queen Hatshepsut became his **regent**. She made important decisions for him. She became so powerful that she was crowned "king" in 1503 BC. She even wore the pharaoh's ceremonial royal beard.

The mortuary temple of Queen Hatshepsut was cut into solid rock.

KING TUTANKHAMUN

In 1922, an archaeologist named Howard Carter was exploring the Valley of the Kings. He discovered a hidden tomb under a pile of rock. Carter was amazed to find that the tomb was mostly intact. Although it had apparently been broken into in ancient times, only the entrance area had been robbed.

Priceless treasures such as this gold mask were found in King Tut's tomb.

24

3100-30 BC

3250 BC

2686-2181 BC

2500 BC

1570-1200 BC

1503 BC

1361 BC

332-30 BC

The tomb contained the mummy of King Tutankhamun, also known as King Tut. The tomb was packed with treasures including a solid gold coffin, a gold mask, and jewelry.

Not much is known about King Tut. Archaeologists do know that King Tut was only a boy when he came to power in 1361 BC. He died in 1352 BC at the age of 18.

After King Tut's tomb was opened, some of those present died mysteriously. Many believed they had been cursed by King Tut's mummy. Since then, countless movies and stories have been written about the mummy's curse.

25

THE END OF A GREAT EMPIRE

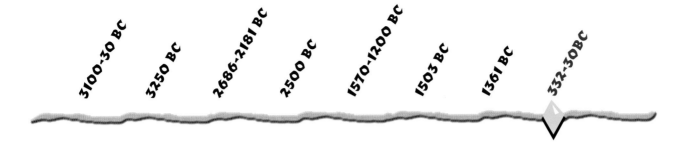

Egypt was invaded by Greece in 332 BC. For the next three hundred years Egypt was controlled by Greek rulers. The last of the Greek rulers was Queen Cleopatra.

At the end of her **reign**, she formed an **alliance** with a Roman leader named Mark Antony. She hoped the alliance would help protect Egypt from the power of the Roman Empire.

Another Roman leader, Octavian, attacked and defeated Mark Antony and Cleopatra's armies. After his defeat, Antony killed himself. Cleopatra tried to form an alliance with Octavian, but failed. Legend has it that she then killed herself by allowing a snake to bite her. Rome conquered Egypt in 30 BC, ending an amazing era of ancient Egyptian dynasties.

Queen Cleopatra died in 30 BC.

TIMELINE

5500 BC - Evidence of first humans to settle and begin farming along the Nile

3100-2686 BC - Early Dynastic Period

2686-2181 BC - The Old Kingdom. Pyramids were built for the pharaohs during this period

2181-2040 BC - 1st intermediate period

3250 BC - First evidence of hieroglyphic writing in Egypt

3100 BC - Egypt is united under king Menes, first king of the first dynasty

2686 BC - First pyramid built for pharaoh Djoser—The Step Pyramid

2040-1782 BC - The Middle Kingdom

28

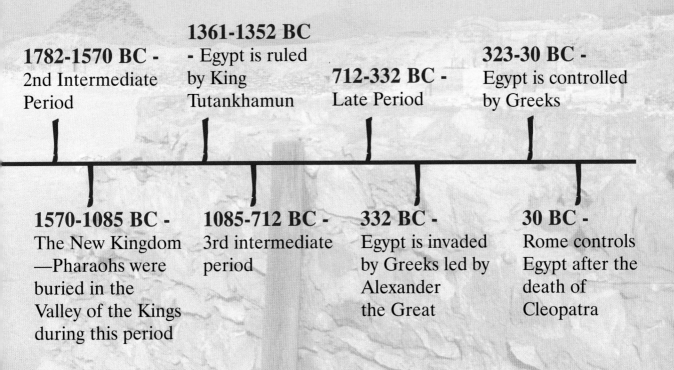

1782-1570 BC -
2nd Intermediate
Period

1361-1352 BC
- Egypt is ruled
by King
Tutankhamun

712-332 BC -
Late Period

323-30 BC -
Egypt is controlled
by Greeks

1570-1085 BC -
The New Kingdom
—Pharaohs were
buried in the
Valley of the Kings
during this period

1085-712 BC -
3rd intermediate
period

332 BC -
Egypt is invaded
by Greeks led by
Alexander
the Great

30 BC -
Rome controls
Egypt after the
death of
Cleopatra

GLOSSARY

alliance (uh LYE uhns) — an agreement to work together

archaeologists (AR kee AHL uh jists) — people who study past human life by examining artifacts left by ancient people

artifacts (ART eh fakts) — objects made or changed by humans

civilizations (siv eh leh ZAY shunz) — highly developed societies

demotic (di MOT ik) — a more simple form of hieratic script

hieratic (HI eh RAT ik) — a short and fast form of writing that joined characters the way cursive writing does

hieroglyphics (hy roh GLIF iks) — a complex system of picture writing

pharaohs (FAIR ohz) — rulers of ancient Egypt

natron (NAY tron) — a salty substance used to preserve dead bodies

regent (REE jent) — a person who rules in the absence of the rightful king or queen

reign (RAYN) — to rule as a king or queen

scribes (SKRYBZ) — public clerks or secretaries in ancient times

PRONUNCIATION GUIDE

Khafra (KAH fruh)
Khufu (KOO foo)
Hatshepsut (haht SHEP sut)
sphinx (SFINKS)
Tutankhamun (toot ahng KAH men)

FURTHER READING

Chrisp, Peter. *Ancient Egypt Revealed*. Dorling
    Kindersley, 2002

Morris, Neil. *The Atlas of Ancient Egypt*. Peter Bedrick
    Books, 2000

Rees, Rosemary. *The Ancient Egyptians*. Heinemann
    Library, 2001

WEBSITES TO VISIT

www.guardians.net/egypt/

www.pbs.org/wgbh/nova/egypt/

www.nationalgeographic.com/pyramids

INDEX

ABOUT THE AUTHORS

David and Patricia Armentrout have written many nonfiction books for young readers. They have had several books published for primary school reading. The Armentrouts live in Cincinnati, Ohio, with their two children.